D0566077

THE TWINKIES® COOKBOOK

THE Twinkies BRAND COOKBOOK

AN INVENTIVE AND UNEXPECTED RECIPE COLLECTION
FROM HOSTESS®

Food photography by Leo Gong

TEN SPEED PRESS
Berkeley | Toronto

Copyright © 2006 by Interstate Bakeries
    Corporation
Food photography copyright © 2005 by Leo Gong
All archival photography copyright © by Interstate
    Bakeries Corporation
Recipe page 10 copyright © by Clare Crespo, author
    of *Hey There, Cupcake!* and *The Secret Life of Food*

All rights reserved. No part of this book may be
reproduced in any form, except brief excerpts for
the purpose of review, without written permission
of the publisher.

Twinkies® and Hostess® are registered trademarks of
Interstate Bakeries Corporation. All rights reserved.

Ten Speed Press
Box 7123
Berkeley, California 94707
www.tenspeed.com

Distributed in Australia by Simon and Schuster
Australia, in Canada by Ten Speed Press Canada,
in New Zealand by Southern Publishers Group,
in South Africa by Real Books, and in the United
Kingdom and Europe by Airlift Book Company.

Cover and text design by Betsy Stromberg
Food styling by Pouké
Food styling assistance by Jeffrey Larsen and
    Christina Milne
Photography assistance by Stacey Lunden and
    Harumi Shimizu
Prop styling by Natalie Hoelen

Library of Congress Cataloging-in-Publication Data
The Twinkies cookbook : an inventive and unex-
pected recipe collection / from Hostess.
    p. cm.
Summary: "The official Twinkies historical refer-
ence and cookbook, with sweet and savory recipes
from fans showcasing the many ingenious ways to
cook with Twinkies"—
Provided by publisher.
Includes index.
ISBN-13: 978-1-58008-756-8 (hardcover)
ISBN-10: 1-58008-756-6 (hardcover)
1. Cake. 2. Desserts. 3. Twinkies (Trademark)
TX771.T85 2006
641.8'653—dc22   2005025316

Printed in China
First printing, 2006

1 2 3 4 5 6 7 8 9 10 — 10 09 08 07 06

CONTENTS

viii ACKNOWLEDGMENTS

ix PREFACE

1 TWINKIES: HISTORY OF A SWEET SENSATION

CHAPTER ONE
NOVELTY TWINKIES

10 Twinkie Sushi

12 Twinkie Train

13 Twinkie Peanut Butter Logs

14 Twinkie Birds

17 Twinkie Pancakes

18 Twinkie Easter Egg Hunt

20 Twinkiehenge

21 French Twinkies

22 Deep-Fried Twinkies with Raspberry Syrup

CHAPTER TWO
TWINKIES FOR CHOCOLATE LOVERS

26 Fried Twinkies with Chocolate Sauce

27 Twinkie-Choconana Toffee Crunch

29 Twinkie Burrito

30 Chocolate Twinkie Trifle

31 Twinkie Éclair

32 Twinkie Petits Fours

34 Chocolate Twinkie Pops

CHAPTER THREE
FRUITY TWINKIES

37 Twinkie Kebabals

38 Twinkie Strawberry Shortcake

40 Twinkie Fantasy

41 Twinkie Orange Bavarian Dream

43 Twinkie Cherry Pie

44 Pineapple Twinkie Pudding

CHAPTER FOUR
TWINKIES TAKE THE CAKE

46 Ribbons and Bows Twinkie Wedding Cake

50 Easy Twinkie Peach Cake

51 Twinkie Macchiato Cake

53 Twinkie Tunnel Bundt Cake

54 Twinkie Cheesecake with Cherry Topping

55 Twinkie Icebox Cake

CHAPTER FIVE
TWINKIES À LA MODE

58 Banana Frozen Yogurt Twinkie Sundae

59 Twinkie Ice Cream Cake

60 Twinkie Banana Split

63 Twinkie Bomb

64 Twinkie Ice Cream

66 Grandma Jo's Twinkie Jell-O Dessert

CHAPTER SIX
TWINKIE DRINKS

68 Twinkie Love Potion Number 75

69 Twinkie Milkshake

70 Twinkie Grasshopper

CHAPTER SEVEN
TWINKIE STACK-UPS

75 Patriotic Twinkie Pie

77 Peanut Butter and Jelly
    Twinkie Cake

78 Strawberry Twinkie Stack

80 Twinkie Lasagna

82 Trifle in the Twinkie of an Eye

CHAPTER EIGHT
GOURMET TWINKIES

84 Twinkie-Misu

87 Banana Twinkie Bread Pudding

88 Twinkie-Pecan Bananas Foster

90 Pumpkin Twinkie Bread Pudding

CHAPTER NINE
TWINKIES AND MEAT

95 Chicken-Raspberry Twinkie Salad

97 Pigs in a Twinkie

98 Twinkling Turkey

100 **INDEX**

ACKNOWLEDGMENTS

Interstate Bakeries Corporation (IBC), the maker of Hostess® Twinkies®, would like to thank the following individuals and organizations for making this special recipe collection possible:

Tony Alvarez and Jacques Roizen of Alvarez & Marsal for bringing their keen business insights and marketing savvy to IBC and for helping to ensure a bright future for one of America's greatest brands;

Hannah Arnold, who conceived this book and wrote the introduction chronicling the role of Twinkies in our history and society, and the team at Linden Alschuler & Kaplan, Inc. Public Relations;

Theresa Cogswell, Kevin Kaul, and all of the dedicated IBC employees who devoted their time and talents to this unique project;

Kathy Moore and Roxanne Wyss of Electrified Cooks for expertly testing—and tasting—these exciting recipes; and

Holly Taines White, managing editor of Ten Speed Press, who recognized this project's potential from the beginning and gave it wholehearted support and skillful editing.

PREFACE

For more than seventy-five years, Twinkies have tantalized the taste buds of the young and old alike with a sweet and irresistible charm. We used to think the golden crème-filled sponge cake just couldn't get any better, until a nationwide search for Twinkie-inspired recipes proved us wrong.

We want to thank the hundreds of Twinkie enthusiasts who opened up their recipe boxes to make this special book possible. From Twinkie-Misu to Twinkie Burritos to Twinkie-Pecan Bananas Foster, this collection features the best-of-the-best easy and delicious Twinkie creations from America's kitchens. Dig in!

—Interstate Bakeries Corporation, maker of Hostess® Twinkies®

 IX

Hostess **TWINKIES** give your customers a real one-two ... and they love it!

Num-ber One! Hostess Twinkies are just great ... by themselves. As dessert, as a treat in a lunch box, as a between-meal snack ... your customers love Twinkies ... and then some!

Num-ber Two! Hostess Twinkies are just great ... served with fruit ... with ice cream. Matter of fact, housewives have told us their families eat even more of these favorite desserts when Twinkies are perched on the side of plates!

So ... it's just good old-fashioned horse sense to get Hostess Twinkies out in plain view ... on your counter. That's where Twinkies will really go to work for you ... selling those related items day-in, day-out! Yes, Twinkies have *earned* their reputation as one of the biggest-little-sales-pluggers in the grocery business, today!

Continental Baking Company, Inc.

THEY'RE CREAMED FILLED!

P J 1469

TWINKIES:
HISTORY OF A SWEET SENSATION

What makes Twinkies so special? Everyone has an answer.

Maybe it's their astonishing staying power. Talk about shelf life! If there were a lifetime achievement award for snack cakes, Twinkies would certainly set the gold standard.

Perhaps it's the nostalgia. From comic strips to the silver screen, state fairs to science projects, legal legends to urban legends, artifacts to art exhibits, Howdy Doody to Archie Bunker—Twinkies have been baked into our national pop culture for generations. Who would have thought a simple confection of sponge cake and crème filling could become a national icon?

> "The Twinkie is the perfect postmodern artifact, a pop culture staple."
> —*BALTIMORE SUN*, 1997

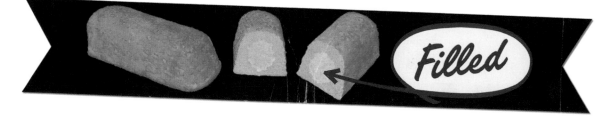

Filled

Tell your troubles

Of course, one wonders if a few persistent tall tales have had a little something to do with the timeless mystique. For the record, Twinkies don't last forever—only about twenty-five days. Nor are they made with a supersecret chemical compound that makes them indestructible. Contrary to what Homer may have been told in a memorable episode of *The Simpsons*, you *can* harm a Twinkie.

Maybe it's old-fashioned national pride. As a vintage television spot declared, "Twinkies are American through and through." President Clinton certainly must have thought so when he chose the Twinkie as an "object of enduring American symbolism" for the National Millennium Time Capsule. It's a good bet Twinkies will still be around when that capsule resurfaces—although we wouldn't recommend eating one after it's been buried.

But why overthink it? After all, we're talking about Twinkies here. Have you tasted one lately? They're incredibly good. If it's been a while, your first bite will undoubtedly be even sweeter than you remembered. Diet mavens may balk, but at 150 calories per Twinkie, you could do a lot worse these days.

Whatever the root of their appeal, Twinkies sparkle with an undeniable magic—a star that seems to shine brighter with age. This is quite astonishing considering the snack cake's inventor was just looking for a way to put idle shortcake pans to use when strawberries were out of season.

> "When it's between my career or a Twinkie, the Twinkie always wins."
> —FORMER *SEINFELD* STAR JASON ALEXANDER, *US*, 1996

* * *

Twinkies' remarkably colorful history dates back to early 1930. Hoovervilles were sprouting from state to state, astronomers had just discovered the planet Pluto, the Chrysler Building neared completion in New York, and bakery manager James A. Dewar was embarking on the "best darn-tootin' idea" he ever had.

Ten years after starting his career driving a horse-drawn pound cake wagon for the Continental Baking Company outside Chicago, Dewar was at the frontier of almost unimaginable fame. Continental was looking for a new, inexpensive product that would appeal to frugal consumers in the tight economy. Why not use the company's stockpile of shortcake pans to create a treat that could be sold year-round? Dewar thought.

Blending a dry mix of necessity, practicality, and ingenuity, he whipped up the celebrated recipe by injecting smooth and creamy banana filling into the oblong golden finger cakes. Unlike strawberries, which were only in season for six weeks during the summer, bananas were readily available year-round.

As for the name, a St. Louis billboard advertising "Twinkle Toe Shoes" provided all the inspiration Dewar needed. He was quoted as saying he "shortened it to make it a little zippier for the kids."

Dewar's new two-for-a-nickel treat was an instant hit.

"To think [Continental] didn't know if people would like them," recalled Margaret Branco, one of the company's original "Twinkie stuffers," in an interview with the *St. Louis Post-Dispatch*. "We could hardly keep up with the demand. You'd think people had nothing to do but eat Twinkies. They sold like hotcakes."

> "Twinkies are warm, Twinkies are cuddly, Twinkies always bring a smile to one's face and put a gleam in one's eyes. The Twinkie has long been a symbol of American pride."
>
> —MINNESOTA RESIDENT LISA KRANZ, *WALL STREET JOURNAL*, 1976

In the early days, every Twinkie had to be hand filled using a specially created machine operated with a foot pedal. "You had to pump the pedal just right, or too much filling would shoot out," Branco explained. "If I oversquirted, the Twinkie would explode. Of course, that wasn't so bad. I got to eat the cripples ones. I never lost my appetite for them. Not only that, I lost weight. I was a butterball when I started. I got thinner on Twinkies."

As Twinkies marched to snack cake superstardom, Dewar, like a proud parent, remained their number one fan, eating at least three a day for more than fifty years. (He admitted to having "sort of a sweet tooth.")

Dewar's grandchildren, in an interview with the *Rochester Democrat and Chronicle,* recalled how "Grandpa Twinkie" never tired of telling the Twinkie story and would regularly visit grocery stores to make sure the little cakes were always fresh. He kept his own stash in the fridge and freezer.

"Some people say Twinkies are the quintessential junk food, but I believe in the things," Dewar once told *United Press*

> "Deep down, I always preferred a package of Twinkies . . . to a handful of natural oats. Given a choice, so would a horse."
>
> —FORMER *CHICAGO DAILY NEWS* COLUMNIST MIKE ROYKO, *WALL STREET JOURNAL,* 1976

International. "I fed them to my four kids and they feed them to my fifteen grandchildren. Twinkies never hurt them."

Though Twinkies became one of the most popular products in American history, Dewar reportedly never received any special compensation for his illustrious invention. He retired from Continental in 1972, having become a vice president. But no promotion could ever have topped his title as "Mr. Twinkie."

After Dewar's death in 1985 at age eighty-eight, a Shelbyville, Indiana, man emerged to stake claim to top Twinkie-eating honors. Ninety-year-old Lewis Browning, a retired milk truck driver, said he has eaten at least one Twinkie a day since 1941. That's right, more than twenty thousand Twinkies.

Browning's snack cake love affair started on the job. Before setting out on his daily twenty-five-mile trip from the farm to the dairy, Browning would pick up a treat for the road. At first, he was a Hostess cupcake man. But the gooey chocolate icing became too much to handle in transit on the bumpy dirt roads.

"Back in the old days, trucks didn't have power steering," Browning recalled. "After eating cupcakes, I'd have black icing all over me by the time I got to the dairy. I decided to just eat Twinkies on the way in so I wouldn't have to clean up before unloading my milk. I just made it a habit."

With his milk-hauling days a decade behind him (he didn't retire until he was eighty), Browning now enjoys a Twinkie first thing each morning with a banana and a cold glass of milk. Not even a recent stay in intensive care could shake the tradition. Browning's wife of fifty-five years made sure Twinkies were on hand at the hospital and the doctors, happily, approved.

"I ate 'em and gave 'em to all the nurses," he said.

Not everyone has been so obliging when it comes to Twinkies. Take Twinkiegate:

In the 1980s, a grand jury indicted a Minneapolis city council candidate for serving coffee, Kool-Aid, Twinkies, and other sweets to two senior citizens groups. The case led to the passage of the Minnesota Campaign Act, widely known as the Twinkie Law. The seventy-one-year-old candidate, George Belair, lost the election, but the charges against him were eventually dropped.

"How can anyone bribe someone with Twinkies?" he asked in a *Los Angeles Times* article.

Honorable intentions aside, Belair may have seriously underestimated what people would do for a Twinkie—or the raw emotions the little snack cake could evoke.

Just ask *Rocky Mountain News* columnist Mark Wolf. When Hostess experimented with Fruit and Crème Twinkies several years ago, Wolf fired off an irate headline: "Hey Hostess, here's a tip: Don't mess with my Twinkies."

"To alter a Twinkie is to demean a national resource," the self-described Twinkie-holic wrote. "How could anyone tinker with perfection?

> "[The doctor] said it wouldn't hurt me, so I even ate a Twinkie in intensive care."
> —TWINKIE-EATING LEGEND LEWIS BROWNING, *WASHINGTON POST,* 2005

> "The genius of Twinkies is they are exactly what they are—amazingly simple and tres elegantes."
>
> —COOKBOOK AUTHOR JANE STERN, *WASHINGTON POST,* 1985

"Despite occasional attacks by misguided nutritionists and dentists, the original Twinkie reigns as *the* American snack food and arguably the greatest product of the Industrial Revolution."

To be fair, Hostess thought consumers might appreciate a throwback to the shortcake's roots, but ultimately decided to abandon the idea. No doubt to the comfort of legions of Twinkie purists, the fruit and crème effort was a rare occasion in Twinkie history when the classic cake was, well, "messed with."

With the exception of a change to vanilla filling during World War II, driven by a banana shortage, and the introduction of a "light" variety in 1990, Twinkies have remained remarkably close to the original recipe. And that's just the way people like it—to the tune of five hundred million Twinkies each year.

So let us raise a toast to an American original—the magical, mystifying, magnificent Twinkie.

The journey's been quite a treat.

CHAPTER ONE

NOVELTY
TWINKIES

TWINKIE SUSHI

66 *I often use Hostess products in my crazy food recipes. They're a great art supply. I love sushi and thought it would be fun to have sushi for dessert. It's nice to serve Twinkie Sushi at a dinner party on a Japanese tray or bento box with chopsticks. Guests will laugh while they enjoy a refreshing fruity dessert at the same time.* 99

CLARE CRESPO, BATON ROUGE, LOUISIANA

SERVES 6

4 pieces green fruit leather, sliced into 1-inch-wide strips

6 Twinkies, cut into 1-inch pieces

Assorted dried fruits, cut into small pieces

Assorted chewy fruity candies

4 to 6 pieces of dried mango, cut into strips

One at a time, wrap the fruit leather pieces around the Twinkie pieces. Place the wrapped Twinkies upright on a serving tray or in a bento box.

Place the dried fruits and candies into the crème filling. Garnish the tray with strips of dried mango to resemble pickled ginger. Serve with chopsticks if you wish.

TWINKIE TRAIN

This Hostess original recipe is perfect for holiday family fun.

SERVES 4

5 Twinkies

1/2 cup white frosting

16 peppermint starlight candies

3 (21/2-inch) pieces red shoestring licorice

1 chocolate kiss

1 miniature chocolate-covered peanut butter cup

3 or 4 animal crackers

Variety of small, colorful hard candies such as gumdrops, chocolate stars, red- and green-coated chocolate candies, or other holiday candies

Place 4 Twinkies in a straight line on a decorative tray or serving plate. Use frosting to attach 4 peppermint candies to each Twinkie as wheels. Stick the licorice pieces between the cars to connect them.

For the engine, cut a 1- to 11/2-inch piece off the remaining Twinkie. Using frosting as glue, attach the piece to the top of the front car, with the cut end even with the back of the bottom Twinkie and the rounded end facing forward. Using frosting, attach the candy kiss atop the engine at the front edge. Using frosting, attach the peanut butter cup to the very front of the engine.

Gently cut a 3-inch slice off the top center of each of the 3 Twinkies behind the engine, exposing the crème filling. Fill 1 car with animal crackers, standing them upright. Fill the other 2 cars with the candies of your choice.

TWINKIE PEANUT BUTTER LOGS

66 *My recipe is a whim based on a frozen* pâte à choux *dessert I used to make at a café where I was a chef. It can be served resting on a pool of chocolate sauce, topped with whipped cream or ice cream, or eaten alone.* 99

DONALD GARRITANO, CEDAR PARK, TEXAS

SERVES 4

4 Twinkies, still wrapped

1/4 cup butter, at room temperature

1/4 cup peanut butter or other nut butter

1/4 cup maple syrup

1/4 cup unsweetened cocoa powder

Freeze the Twinkies for about 1 hour, or until firm.

Combine the butter, peanut butter, maple syrup, and cocoa powder in a microwave-safe bowl. Microwave on high power for 30 seconds, or until warm. Stir to blend well.

Unwrap the Twinkies and slice in half lengthwise. Spoon about 2 tablespoons of the peanut butter mixture into the center of each Twinkie. Reassemble the Twinkies and place on plastic wrap. Divide the remaining peanut butter mixture evenly on top of the Twinkies and frost the tops and sides. Wrap the Twinkies in the plastic wrap and freeze for 6 to 8 hours. To serve, cut in the Twinkies in half horizontally. Serve frozen, ideally on chilled or frozen plates.

TWINKIE BIRDS

" *We're a Twinkie family—we'd rather eat Twinkies than anything else. I'm also always trying to find something to amuse my three grandchildren, and that's what led to this idea. I'm a grandma with too much time on her hands!* "

DIANNE MEYERS, LAKEMOOR, ILLINOIS

SERVES 10

10 Twinkies
1 cup milk chocolate chips
1 tablespoon salted butter
20 mini semisweet chocolate chips
30 pieces candy corn
5 chocolate sandwich cookies

Line a baking sheet with waxed paper. Slice off a thin layer from one end of each Twinkie so they can sit upright.

Combine the milk chocolate chips and butter in a small, microwave-safe bowl and microwave on high power for 30 seconds. Stir, then continue to microwave in 10- to 15-second increments, until melted and smooth. Allow to cool slightly.

Dip the bottom and sides of each Twinkie in the melted chocolate, leaving the top and a 3/4-inch strip down the center of the Twinkie uncovered, so as to resemble the markings of a penguin. Stand the Twinkies upright on the prepared baking sheet and let sit for 1 hour, or until the chocolate is set. Reserve the remaining melted chocolate.

Using a toothpick, lightly poke 2 mini chocolate chips into each Twinkie to form eyes. For beaks, slightly flatten 10 candy corns and poke the wide ends into the Twinkies.

Twist open the cookies and scrape away and discard the cream filling. Cut each cookie in half. Use a small amount of the melted chocolate to attach half a cookie on each side of the Twinkies as wings, positioning the cookies with the cut edge facing forward. (If necessary, remelt the chocolate in the microwave for 10 to 15 seconds.)

For feet, slightly flatten the remaining 20 candy corns. Push the tips of 2 candy corns into each Twinkie at the base.

TWINKIE PANCAKES

66 *This recipe was inspired by Shrek Twinkies, which were made with green filling and in stores when the movie came out on DVD. One night I had a Shrek movie party for my grandkids. The next morning I wanted to make something memorable for breakfast, so I created Twinkie pancakes. The kids said the green color spots made them look really cool.* 99

JERRY FERRILL, COLUMBUS, OHIO

SERVES 4 TO 6

6 Twinkies

4 cups prepared pancake batter

Butter or margarine, for serving (optional)

Pancake syrup, for serving (optional)

Slice each Twinkie crosswise into 8 thin slices. Spray a griddle or skillet with nonstick vegetable oil spray or brush lightly with vegetable oil. Heat the griddle over medium-high heat.

Pour 1/4-cup measures of the pancake batter onto the hot griddle, spacing them apart. Arrange 3 Twinkie slices in each pancake. Cook until the pancake begins to bubble and is golden brown on the underside. Carefully turn the pancakes and cook the second side. Serve immediately with butter and syrup.

TWINKIE EASTER EGG HUNT

" I've always been a loyal Twinkie fan. I originally came up with this recipe as a way to get our children seated and quieted down after they finished their Easter egg hunt. It's become a family tradition. By changing the food coloring and decorations, you can use it to make something special for any holiday. "

MAXINE FRANK, CLEARWATER, FLORIDA

SERVES 10 TO 15

10 Twinkies

Spray food coloring in a
    variety of colors

3 (7-ounce) jars marsh-
    mallow crème

20 maraschino cherries,
    well drained

6 ounces semisweet chocolate
    chips

1/2 cup jelly beans

1 (5.9-ounce) package instant
    chocolate pudding mix

3 cups milk

Spray the Twinkies with the food coloring, using a variety of colors. Cut each Twinkie in half crosswise.

Spoon the marshmallow crème into a 9 by 13-inch baking dish, covering the bottom completely. Arrange the Twinkies cut side down in the crème, leaving the tops sticking up out of the crème so they look like Easter eggs. Decorate around the Twinkies with the maraschino cherries, chocolate chips, and jelly beans.

In a bowl, combine the pudding mix and milk and stir according to the package instructions. Chill until thickened.

To serve, spoon 3 to 4 tablespoons of the pudding into each bowl. Scoop up a Twinkie along with some of the marshmallow crème and candies and add to each bowl.

TWINKIEHENGE

    Some believe Twinkiehenge was created as an archaic sundial, designed to provide my ancestors with the precise time to serve and eat dessert. But this theory is widely refuted, as even casual observers can see that any time is considered the right time for dessert in the Brakeville clan. Twinkiehenge is a great dessert for relatives and supreme alien beings alike.

BARRY BRAKEVILLE, LENEXA, KANSAS

SERVES 4

- 1 (5.9-ounce) package instant chocolate pudding mix
- 3 cups milk
- 12 to 16 chocolate sandwich cookies, crushed into fine crumbs
- 3 to 4 Twinkies, halved crosswise

In a bowl, combine the pudding mix and milk and stir according to the package instructions, until thickened. Pour the pudding into a serving bowl.

Sprinkle the crushed cookies over the pudding, covering the surface completely. Plunge the Twinkies pieces cut side down into the pudding, arranging them in a circle with the rounded edges protruding from the pudding.

FRENCH TWINKIES

❝❝ *This tasty snack is surprisingly easy to make and sure to bring a smile to even the grumpiest little ones in the morning. I like to prepare it on special occasions, such as birthday breakfasts.* **❞❞**

JANINE O'BARR, BURBANK, CALIFORNIA

SERVES 4

2 tablespoons butter

4 Twinkies

2 eggs, lightly beaten

Pancake syrup or
    confectioners' sugar,
    for serving

Melt the butter in a skillet over medium heat. Dip each Twinkie into the beaten eggs, coating evenly. Immediately place the Twinkies in the hot skillet and cook until lightly browned and crispy on each side, turning to cook evenly. Serve warm, drizzled with syrup or dusted with confectioners' sugar.

DEEP-FRIED TWINKIES WITH RASPBERRY SYRUP

❝ *Make sure to serve the Twinkies warm. They're incredibly rich, so enjoy them sparingly.* ❞

DIANE BULTEMEIER, OCEANSIDE, CALIFORNIA

SERVES 6

6 Twinkies

Vegetable oil, for deep-frying

1 cup milk

2 tablespoons cider vinegar

1 tablespoon vegetable oil

1 cup all-purpose flour, plus more for dusting

1 teaspoon baking powder

1/2 teaspoon salt

Raspberry syrup, for serving

Confectioners' sugar, for serving (optional)

Freeze the Twinkies for several hours or overnight.

Pour the frying oil into a deep fryer or saucepan. It should be deep enough for the Twinkies to be submerged. Heat on high or over high heat until the oil reaches 375°F.

In a large bowl, combine the milk, vinegar, and oil and mix well. In a small bowl, combine the flour, baking powder, and salt. Stir the flour mixture into the milk mixture, blending until smooth.

Dust the Twinkies lightly with flour, then dip into the batter, coating evenly and allowing the excess to drip off.

Carefully place 1 or 2 Twinkies in the hot oil without crowding them. Fry for about 45 seconds on each side, turning to brown evenly. (Carefully use tongs or a long spoon to push the Twinkies down into the oil so they brown evenly.) Remove and drain on paper towels. Repeat with the remaining Twinkies. Cool for about 5 minutes, then serve while still warm, drizzled with raspberry syrup and dusted with confectioners' sugar.

CHAPTER TWO

TWINKIES
FOR CHOCOLATE LOVERS

FRIED TWINKIES WITH CHOCOLATE SAUCE

" I came up with this dessert one night after discovering I was out of the ice cream balls I use to make fried ice cream, one of my favorite desserts. I grabbed some Twinkies I had in the cabinet as a substitute and, wow, were they great. Now, whenever I have a cookout or a group of friends over, I serve chocolate fried Twinkies. "

KARL E. MOSER, CONWAY, SOUTH CAROLINA

SERVES 4

About 4 cups vegetable oil, for deep-frying

4 Twinkies

1/4 cup confectioners' sugar

Chocolate syrup

Whipped cream, for garnish (optional)

Pour the oil into a deep fryer or saucepan. It should be deep enough to half cover a Twinkie. Heat on high or over high heat until the oil reaches 375°F.

Carefully place 1 or 2 of the Twinkies in the hot oil without crowding them. Fry for about 20 seconds on each side, turning to brown evenly. Remove and drain on paper towels. Repeat with the remaining Twinkies. Allow the Twinkies to cool briefly.

Place each Twinkie on a small dessert plate and dust with the confectioners' sugar. Drizzle with chocolate syrup, garnish with whipped cream, and serve at once.

TWINKIE-CHOCONANA TOFFEE CRUNCH

I recently got married, and the big joke is that I only know how to make reservations. So this recipe was a surprising breakthrough. Chocolate and banana is my favorite combination, and I thought it would be awesome to add a Twinkie to my favorite blend of flavors. If I do say so myself, it's delicious!

MICHELE ISBRECHT GREENBAUM, EAST NORRITON, PENNSYLVANIA

SERVES 12

10 Twinkies, halved lengthwise

1 (22-ounce) container prepared chocolate pudding

4 bananas, sliced

1 (6.5-ounce) can chocolate whipped cream

2/3 cup milk chocolate English toffee bits

Arrange half of the Twinkies cut side up in a 9 by 13-inch baking dish.

Spread one-third of the pudding over the Twinkies, covering completely. Arrange half of the banana slices in single layer over the pudding. Repeat the layering with the remaining Twinkie halves, another one-third of the pudding, and the remaining banana slices. Spread the remaining pudding over the top of the bananas.

Decorate the entire surface with the whipped cream and sprinkle the toffee bits over the top.

TWINKIE BURRITO

66 *I have always loved Twinkies with chocolate and strawberries. One day while at my wife's Mexican restaurant, I tried wrapping the mixture in a tortilla so I could eat it with my hands. Even though my wife laughs at me, Twinkie burritos are delicious, and now all of her employees and I are hooked!* 99

PETER SHERIDAN, WASHINGTON, D.C.

SERVES 4

4 (10- to 12-inch) flour
   tortillas, warmed

1/2 to 3/4 cup chocolate sauce

4 Twinkies

2 cups sliced strawberries,
   or 1/2 cup strawberry
   preserves

Drizzle one side of each tortilla with the chocolate sauce. Place a Twinkie on top of the chocolate sauce in the center of each tortilla. Top each Twinkie with 1/4 cup of the strawberries. Fold the tortillas over the Twinkies and roll up like a burrito.

CHOCOLATE TWINKIE TRIFLE

" I got the idea for this recipe after my wife made a trifle for a special occa-sion. I thought chocolate would go well with Twinkies and the whipped topping would be light enough to reduce the sweetness. Everyone enjoyed the dessert . . . after all, how can one not enjoy a Twinkie? "

PETER HALFERTY, CORPUS CHRISTI, TEXAS

SERVES 12 TO 15

20 Twinkies

1 (5.9-ounce) package instant chocolate pudding mix

3 cups milk

1/2 cup chocolate syrup

1 (12-ounce) container frozen nondairy whipped topping, thawed

6 (1.4-ounce) milk chocolate English toffee candy bars, finely chopped

Cut 10 of the Twinkies in half lengthwise and arrange standing upright, filling side in, around a 4-quart trifle bowl or a deep glass bowl.

In a bowl, combine the pudding mix and milk and stir according to the package instructions.

Crumble the remaining 10 Twinkies, reserving 1/2 cup for the topping. Place half of the Twinkie crumbs in the bottom of the trifle bowl. Layer with half of the chocolate syrup, half of the pudding, half of the whipped topping, and half of the crushed candy bars. Repeat the layers of Twinkie crumbs, syrup, pudding, and whipped topping.

Combine the remaining crushed candy bars with the reserved 1/2 cup Twinkie crumbs and sprinkle over the trifle. Refrigerate for 4 to 5 hours before serving.

TWINKIE ÉCLAIR

" This recipe was given to me by my grandmother, except her version called for ladyfingers. As I was making it one night, I realized that I didn't have ladyfingers, but a frantic search through the pantry turned up my husband's Twinkies. He was a little sad not to have the Twinkies for lunch, but we loved the new version of Grandma's dessert. In fact, we never made it the old way again. "

LORI KIMBLE, MASCOUTAH, ILLINOIS

SERVES 9

10 Twinkies, halved lengthwise

1 (3.4-ounce) package instant vanilla pudding mix

2 cups milk

1 (8-ounce) container frozen nondairy whipped topping, thawed

1 (16-ounce) container chocolate frosting

Arrange half of the Twinkies cut side up in an 8 by 8-inch baking dish.

In a bowl, combine the pudding mix and milk and stir according to the package instructions. Fold in the whipped topping. Spread the pudding mixture over the Twinkies. Arrange the remaining Twinkies cut side down over the pudding.

Remove the cover and foil seal from the frosting container and microwave on high power for 1 minute. Stir well, then drizzle the frosting over the Twinkies. Refrigerate for 1 hour, or until firm.

TWINKIE PETITS FOURS

" *I created this recipe in honor of my dad, using his favorite treats—Twinkies and chocolate. They are so good, and no one believes me when I tell them what they are.* *"*

BARBARA CANFIELD, BAKERSFIELD, CALIFORNIA

SERVES 4

2 Twinkies

4 ounces milk or dark chocolate (or 1 cup chips), or both

Whipped cream

4 maraschino cherries, halved

Freeze the Twinkies for 1 hour, until firm. Line a baking sheet with waxed paper.

Slice each Twinkie crosswise into 3/4-inch pieces. Place the chocolate in a small, microwave-safe bowl and microwave on high power for 30 seconds. (If you're using both milk and dark chocolates, melt them in separate bowls.) Stir, then continue to microwave for 15 to 30 seconds at a time, stirring frequently, until melted and smooth.

Dip each piece of Twinkie into the melted chocolate, then place on the prepared baking sheet. Decorate the tops of some of the petits fours with swirls or drizzles of the other color of chocolate. Place in the freezer for at least 5 minutes, until firm.

Top the undecorated petit fours with a dollop of whipped cream and a cherry half. Serve immediately.

CHOCOLATE TWINKIE POPS

66 *This recipe was a special treat that I used to prepare with my nana. We enjoyed it in the winter along with a mug of hot chocolate.* 99

LORI BIANCHET, MILLER PLACE, NEW YORK

SERVES 10

10 Twinkies
1 pound dark chocolate

Insert a Popsicle stick lengthwise into each Twinkie, leaving approximately 1 inch of the stick exposed. Place on waxed paper and freeze 3 to 4 hours or overnight.

Prepare a double boiler over simmering water. Line a baking sheet with waxed paper. Melt the chocolate in the double boiler. Dip each Twinkie into the chocolate, turning to coat completely, then place on the prepared baking sheet. Freeze the Twinkie pops for another 3 to 4 hours, until set.

CHAPTER THREE

FRUITY
TWINKIES

TWINKIE KEBABALS

> 66 This was a spur-of-the-moment idea. I had leftover fruit, but not enough Twinkies to give each of the gals at my candle-making party her own. This recipe saved the day. 99

DIANNE MEYERS, LAKEMOOR, ILLINOIS

SERVES 10

10 Twinkies

20 large marshmallows

About 60 pieces or chunks of fruit, such as pitted cherries, pineapple chunks, and mandarin orange slices

Cut each Twinkie crosswise into quarters. Thread alternating pieces of Twinkies, marshmallows, and fruit onto wooden skewers. Serve at once.

TWINKIE STRAWBERRY SHORTCAKE

66 *When my sister-in-law made this recipe for a family dinner, everyone thought she had worked her tail off in the kitchen. She shared the secret of this quick and easy dessert only with the women. Now it's become our inside joke when we make it—the men think we've slaved away for them.* 99

DEBBIE JOHNSTON, SAINT AUGUSTINE, FLORIDA

SERVES 12

10 Twinkies, halved
  lengthwise

1 (16-ounce) package frozen
  strawberries in syrup,
  refrigerated until just
  thawed

1 (8-ounce) container frozen
  nondairy whipped
  topping, thawed

Arrange half of the Twinkies cut side up in a 9 by 13-inch baking dish. Top with half of the strawberries, then half of the whipped topping. Repeat the layers of Twinkies, strawberries, and whipped topping. Cover and refrigerate until chilled, about 1 hour. Cut into squares and serve.

TWINKIE FANTASY

❝ *I developed this recipe just using what I had on hand, substituting Twinkies for cake. Eat a hearty portion or apply liberally to hips and inner thighs!* ❞

JO WARRENFELTZ, EDWARDSVILLE, ILLINOIS

SERVES 12

14 Twinkies

1 (6-ounce) package strawberry Jell-O

1 cup boiling water

1 cup cold water

1 (10-ounce) bag frozen strawberries, thawed

2 (3.4-ounce) packages instant vanilla pudding mix

3 cups milk

1 (8-ounce) container frozen nondairy whipped topping, thawed

Arrange the Twinkies in a 9 by 13-inch baking dish.

In a bowl, combine the Jell-O and boiling water and stir until fully dissolved. Stir in the cold water, cover, and refrigerate for 15 minutes, until partially set. Stir in the strawberries, then pour the Jell-O mixture over the Twinkies. Cover and refrigerate for 1 hour, until set.

In a bowl, combine the pudding mix and milk and stir according to the package instructions. Pour the pudding over the Jell-O and Twinkies. Cover and refrigerate for 1 hour, until set.

Spread the whipped topping evenly on top of the pudding. Cover and refrigerate 2 to 3 hours, until set. Cut into squares and serve immediately.

TWINKIE ORANGE BAVARIAN DREAM

" I've made this dessert using various flavors of Jell-O, but this particular version was inspired by my stepmother, who loves the combination of orange and vanilla and often reminisces about eating Dreamsicles as a girl. "

ANNA GINSBERG, AUSTIN, TEXAS

SERVES 12

- 10 Twinkies, halved lengthwise
- 1 (15-ounce) can mandarin oranges, drained
- 1 (3-ounce) package orange Jell-O
- 1/2 cup boiling water
- 1 (3.4-ounce) package instant French vanilla pudding mix
- 1 1/2 cups milk
- 1/2 cup French vanilla liquid coffee creamer
- 1 (12-ounce) container frozen nondairy whipped topping, thawed

Arrange the Twinkies cut side up in a 9 by 13-inch baking dish. Layer half of the mandarin oranges over the Twinkies.

In a bowl, combine the Jell-O and boiling water and stir to dissolve. Cover and refrigerate for 10 minutes to cool.

In a large bowl, beat together the pudding mix, milk, and coffee creamer for 2 minutes, or until slightly thickened. Add the Jell-O to the pudding mixture and stir until smooth. Fold in two-thirds of the whipped topping until combined. Spread the mixture over the Twinkies and oranges. Cover and refrigerate for 6 to 8 hours, until set.

Just before serving, spread the remaining whipped topping over the top. Decorate with the remaining oranges and cut into squares to serve.

TWINKIE CHERRY PIE

❝ Friends and family love my Twinkie Pie. I make it for barbecues, birthdays, and other special occasions. ❞

CAROLYN NICHOLSON, INGLEWOOD, CALIFORNIA

SERVES 12

1 (8-ounce) package cream cheese, at room temperature

1 (14-ounce) can sweetened condensed milk

10 Twinkies, halved lengthwise

1 (21-ounce) can cherry or other fruit pie filling

1 (15-ounce) can crushed pineapple in juice, drained

1/2 cup chopped Brazil nuts or other nuts (optional)

1 (8-ounce) container frozen nondairy whipped topping, thawed

In a bowl, combine the cream cheese and condensed milk and beat with an electric mixer on medium-high speed until smooth. Arrange the Twinkies cut side up in a 9 by 13-inch baking dish. Pour the cream cheese mixture over the Twinkies.

Reserve about 1 tablespoon of the pie filling for garnish. Spoon the remaining pie filling over the cream cheese layer. Spoon the pineapple over the pie filling.

Reserve 2 tablespoons of the nuts for garnish. Sprinkle the remaining nuts over the pineapple, then spread the whipped topping over all. Garnish with the reserved pie filling and nuts.

Cover and refrigerate for 4 to 6 hours or overnight. Cut into squares to serve.

PINEAPPLE TWINKIE PUDDING

It's a good thing you can always count on my family having a Twinkie in the house or in the glove compartment of the car. One day we had a surprise guest for dinner and I needed a side dish to go with a pork loin. Twinkies came to the rescue in this recipe. It was a real winner. Since then, I've been known as the Twinkie Lady.

DIANA GONYA, BALTIMORE, MARYLAND

SERVES 8

6 Twinkies

2 eggs, lightly beaten

1 cup drained canned
    crushed pineapple in juice

1/4 cup butter or margarine,
    cut into pieces

Preheat the oven to 350°F. Butter a 9-inch pie pan and dust with flour.

Tear each Twinkie into 6 pieces and place in a bowl. Add the beaten eggs and mix gently to coat. Blend in the pineapple and butter, then spoon into the prepared pan.

Place in the oven and bake for 30 to 35 minutes, until lightly browned. Allow to stand for 5 minutes before serving.

CHAPTER FOUR

TWINKIES
TAKE THE CAKE

RIBBONS AND BOWS TWINKIE WEDDING CAKE

This Hostess original recipe is a Twinkie take on a wedding cake. Fondant is a prepared confection, readily available at stores selling cake-decorating supplies, including large craft stores. It comes in a variety of colors and in various package sizes. To use it, place it on a board lightly dusted with cornstarch or confectioners' sugar and roll it to the desired thickness, usually about 1/8 inch thick, with a rolling pin.

SERVES 27

7³/₄ pounds prepared fondant in 2 colors

27 Twinkies

1 (4-inch-diameter, 4-inch-thick) piece Styrofoam

1 (7-inch-diameter) cardboard cake round, covered with decorative, food-safe aluminum foil

1¹/₂ (16-ounce) cans buttercream frosting

1 (8-inch-diameter, 4-inch-thick) piece Styrofoam

1 (11-inch-diameter) cardboard cake round, covered with decorative, food-safe aluminum foil

Reserve 1 pound of the fondant and roll the rest out to 1/8 inch thick. Wrap 13 of the Twinkies in strips of one of the colors of fondant (3¹/₂ to 4 ounces fondant per Twinkie). Lightly brush the edges of the fondant with water to seal tightly. Wrap the remaining 14 Twinkies in the other color of fondant.

For the top layer, place the 4-inch round of Styrofoam in the center of the 7-inch cardboard round. Frost the top and sides with one-third of one can of frosting. Alternating the colors, arrange 10 of the fondant-wrapped Twinkies upright around the Styrofoam, attaching them with the frosting, with the seams facing in. The top edge of the Twinkies should be even with the top of the frosted Styrofoam.

For the bottom layer, place the 8-inch round of Styrofoam in the center of the 11-inch cardboard round. Frost the top and sides with the remaining two-thirds of the first can of frosting. Alternating the colors, arrange the remaining 17 fondant-wrapped Twinkies upright around the Styrofoam, attaching them with the frosting, with the seams facing in. The top edge of the Twinkies should be even with the top of the frosted Styrofoam.

Fill a pastry bag fitted with a #12 tip for larger decorations (or a #4 or #5 tip for more delicate decorations) with frosting. Pipe a decorative filigree of frosting on the top edges of the Twinkies on the bottom layer, or mold fondant into decorative shapes and position on top of the Twinkies.

Stack the top layer on the bottom layer. Fit the pastry bag with a #6 tip. Pipe dots of frosting around the edges of the cardboard circles.

Cut flowers from the fondant with a small cookie cutter and decorate the tops of the Twinkies on the top layer. Fit the pastry bag with a #3 tip and pipe a small dot of frosting in the center of each flower.

To make a bow on top of the cake, roll the reserved 1 pound fondant out to a 1/8-inch thickness and cut into strips about 1 inch wide. Place a generous dollop of frosting on top of the cake, then use a strip of fondant to make a loop, sticking the ends into the frosting to secure. Continue to add loops of fondant ribbon, securing each loop in the frosting, to make a large bow.

EASY TWINKIE PEACH CAKE

❝ When my mother visited us a few years ago, my two daughters wanted to help her make a dessert for the family. My eldest daughter, Danielle, spotted a box of Twinkies in the kitchen and, along with her sister, Mollie, thought up a way to combine it with fruit. My mother added the vanilla sauce to spice things up and lend a little warmth to the dish. ❞

GREGORY SCHAPER, BLUE ASH, OHIO

SERVES 8 TO 10

10 to 12 Twinkies

1 (29-ounce) can sliced peaches, drained

1/2 teaspoon ground cinnamon

1/2 cup sugar

1/2 cup evaporated milk

1/2 cup butter

1 teaspoon pure vanilla extract

Arrange the Twinkies side by side in a 9 by 13-inch baking dish. Cover the Twinkies with the peaches, then sprinkle with the cinnamon.

In a small saucepan, combine the sugar, evaporated milk, and butter. Cook over medium-high heat, stirring constantly, for 4 to 6 minutes, until hot and smooth. Remove from the heat and stir in the vanilla. Pour the sauce over the Twinkies and peaches. Serve warm.

TWINKIE MACCHIATO CAKE

❝ *My husband and I came up with this recipe after being disappointed by a dessert we had while out to dinner. The next day, I created a new version of the restaurant's cake using our favorite crème-filled snack. We both agreed it was a big improvement. I bake plenty of things from scratch and have found that Twinkies make a great ingredient. Why use ladyfingers or plain pound cake when you can use a Twinkie?* ❞

ANNA GINSBERG, AUSTIN, TEXAS

SERVES 12

10 Twinkies, halved lengthwise

2/3 cup caramel ice cream topping

2 tablespoons boiling water

2 tablespoons instant coffee crystals

1 (7-ounce) jar marshmallow crème

1 (12-ounce) container frozen nondairy whipped topping, thawed

1/3 cup chocolate syrup

Arrange the Twinkies cut side up in a 9 by 13-inch baking dish. Drizzle the Twinkies with half of the ice cream topping.

In a large bowl, combine the boiling water and coffee crystals and stir to dissolve. Spoon in the marshmallow crème and stir to soften slightly. Using an electric mixer on high speed, beat until thoroughly combined. Fold in 3 cups of the whipped topping, then spoon the mixture over the Twinkies.

Spread the remaining whipped topping over the top in a light layer. Drizzle with the remaining ice cream topping, then with the chocolate syrup. Refrigerate for at least 3 hours before serving.

TWINKIE TUNNEL BUNDT CAKE

❝ ❝ *I make this cake for special occasions and when company is coming. People love the surprise of finding the Twinkie filling inside the chocolate cake!* ❞ ❞

DARLENE CASALINO, CAPE CORAL, FLORIDA

SERVES 8 TO 12

1 (18.25-ounce) box chocolate cake mix, batter prepared according to package instructions

6 Twinkies, halved lengthwise

Confectioners' sugar, for dusting

Spray a Bundt pan with nonstick vegetable oil spray. Pour half of the cake batter into the prepared pan.

Arrange the Twinkies in a circle in the middle of the batter, cut sides facing out, standing them up vertically so that they are surrounded front and back by the batter. Pour the remainder of the cake batter into the pan. Bake according to the package instructions for cooking with Bundt pans.

Remove from the oven and cool for about 15 minutes in the pan. Invert the pan to remove the cake and transfer to a wire rack to cool completely. Dust the top and sides of the cake with confectioners' sugar and cut into slices to serve.

TWINKIE CHEESECAKE WITH CHERRY TOPPING

> ❝ *I'm always looking for new ways to use my favorite foods, especially when it comes to desserts. A layer of cheesecake on top of a layer of Twinkies makes something special in no time at all. This recipe is a terrific dessert to take to a potluck or church supper.* ❞

LILLIAN JULOW, GAINESVILLE, FLORIDA

SERVES 12

14 Twinkies

1 cup chopped walnuts

3 large eggs

1 (16-ounce) box confectioners' sugar

1 (8-ounce) package cream cheese, at room temperature

1 (30-ounce) can cherry pie filling

Preheat the oven to 350°F. Spray a 9 by 13-inch baking dish with nonstick vegetable oil spray. Arrange the Twinkies side by side in the pan and sprinkle with the walnuts.

In a large bowl, combine the eggs, confectioners' sugar, and cream cheese. Using an electric mixer on medium to high speed, beat until light and fluffy. Spoon dollops of the cream cheese mixture over the Twinkies and carefully smooth to an even layer. Bake for 35 to 40 minutes, until firm and lightly browned.

Transfer the cheesecake to a wire rack and cool to room temperature. Top with the cherry pie filling, spreading it out evenly. Cut into squares to serve.

TWINKIE ICEBOX CAKE

" I've been making this dessert for about eight years, usually for church dinners and family functions. I raised four children by myself and have enjoyed coming up with quick and easy recipes. "

DONALD HARVEY, INDEPENDENCE, MISSOURI

SERVES 12

10 Twinkies

1 (20-ounce) can crushed pineapple in juice, undrained

1 (5.1-ounce) package instant vanilla pudding mix

3 cups milk

1 (8-ounce) container frozen nondairy whipped topping, thawed

1 cup flaked coconut (optional)

Arrange the Twinkies evenly in the bottom of a 9 by 13-inch baking dish. Pour the pineapple, along with its juice, evenly over the Twinkies.

In a bowl, combine the pudding mix and milk and stir according to the package instructions. Immediately pour the pudding over the pineapple. Refrigerate for 1 hour, until chilled.

Gently spread the whipped topping over the pudding and sprinkle with the coconut. Refrigerate overnight before serving.

CHAPTER FIVE

TWINKIES
À LA MODE

BANANA FROZEN YOGURT TWINKIE SUNDAE

> *My parents are from Afghanistan, where yogurt and honey is a popular dessert. It's also one of my favorites. Sometimes we enjoy the yogurt with pound cake, which gave me the idea to use Twinkies to create something similar. This dessert quickly became a favorite of my son and mom.*

SORAYA HAMID, KANSAS CITY, MISSOURI

SERVES 6

1 cup plain yogurt

1 tablespoon freshly squeezed lemon juice

2 tablespoons honey

1/2 teaspoon ground cinnamon

4 large ripe bananas

6 Twinkies

1/2 cup chopped pecans

In a food processor, combine the yogurt, lemon juice, honey, cinnamon, and 3 of the bananas and process until creamy. Pour the mixture into a freezer-safe container and freeze for 30 minutes, until somewhat firm. Put the mixture back into the food processor and process again until ultrasmooth. Return to the freezer for 30 minutes, until firm.

Take the frozen yogurt out of the freezer and let it soften at room temperature for about 10 minutes. Cut the remaining banana into slices. Place 1 Twinkie in each of 6 shallow dessert dishes. Top each with one-sixth of the banana frozen yogurt, then sprinkle with the chopped pecans and banana slices. Serve at once.

TWINKIE ICE CREAM CAKE

> " I have five children who love ice cream cakes, which can be very expensive, so I came up with my own version. This recipe has become a total family favorite. When we have relatives over, they always ask for it, and many of the parents of my children's friends have called for the recipe. "
>
> CAREY BLAKE, OLALLA, WASHINGTON

SERVES 12

CRUST

1½ cups graham cracker crumbs

2 tablespoons confectioners' sugar

6 tablespoons butter, melted

½ gallon chocolate ice cream (in a box), slightly thawed

18 Twinkies

½ gallon vanilla ice cream, at room temperature

½ cup chocolate sauce

1 cup frozen nondairy whipped topping, thawed

Candy sprinkles or toasted chopped nuts, for decorating (optional)

To prepare the crust, combine the cracker crumbs, confectioners' sugar, and melted butter in a bowl and mix well. Transfer to a 9 by 13-inch baking dish and press evenly into the bottom of the dish.

Cut the chocolate ice cream crosswise into 1-inch-thick slices and arrange on top of the crust. Cut 12 of the Twinkies in half lengthwise and arrange cut side down in a single layer over the chocolate ice cream.

Cut the remaining 6 Twinkies into 1-inch pieces and stir into the softened vanilla ice cream. Spread the vanilla ice cream mixture over the Twinkies. Drizzle on the chocolate sauce, then spread with the whipped topping. Decorate with candy sprinkles or nuts.

Freeze for at least 2 hours, until firm. Set out 10 to 15 minutes before serving. Cut into squares to serve.

TWINKIE BANANA SPLIT

My grandma, Memo, and I invented and perfected this recipe a long time ago. Memo is now gone, but the recipe lives on. I work for my dad, who is a farmer and rancher, and this is an easy dessert to prepare at the end of a long day feeding livestock and cultivating thousands of acres of farmland. You can add a 'grown-up' touch by adding rum to the whipped topping.

KAREN ONEY, FORT WORTH, TEXAS

SERVES 4

4 Twinkies

4 bananas, halved lengthwise

1 quart vanilla ice cream

1 (12-ounce) jar strawberry ice cream topping

1 (12-ounce) jar pineapple ice cream topping

1 cup frozen nondairy whipped topping, thawed

1/2 cup chopped cashews

4 maraschino cherries

Place 1 Twinkie in each of 4 banana split dishes and arrange a banana half on either side of each Twinkie. Place 2 small scoops of ice cream with each Twinkie. Top with the strawberry and pineapple toppings and a dollop of whipped topping. Sprinkle on the cashews and top with a cherry. Serve at once.

TWINKIE BOMB

" " *I came up with this recipe for my goddaughter's third birthday. It was a great activity for the kids to take part in—messy and fun.* " "

ZEPHIR PLUME, BOULDER, COLORADO

SERVES 4

6 Twinkies, well chilled

1/2 cup raspberry jam

2 cups vanilla ice cream, at room temperature

Fresh raspberries, for garnish (optional)

Vanilla cream sauce or raspberry dessert sauce, for garnish (optional)

Line 4 parfait dishes with plastic wrap. Cut each Twinkie crosswise into 10 pieces. Arrange a layer of Twinkie pieces in each parfait glass, covering the bottom and sides. Spread the raspberry jam over the Twinkies, filling in any crevices. Spoon the ice cream into the center of each Twinkie-covered parfait. Arrange the remaining Twinkie pieces to completely cover the parfaits. Freeze for about 20 minutes, until firm.

Remove from the freezer and place upside down on dessert plates. Remove the dishes and peel the plastic wrap off each dessert. Garnish with raspberries and vanilla cream sauce and serve at once.

TWINKIE ICE CREAM

> *Two of my favorite desserts have always been Twinkies and ice cream, so I decided to combine them together to create Twinkie ice cream. It tastes wonderful and has been a huge hit at my store, Country Cow Creamery, where we make all of our ice cream, pies, cakes, and other baked goods from scratch.*

EDWARD DUBROWSKI, COLONIA, NEW JERSEY

SERVES 6 TO 8

2 tablespoons all-purpose
    flour

2 tablespoons cold water

2 cups milk

3/4 cup sugar

2 egg yolks, lightly beaten

1 cup heavy whipping cream

1 teaspoon pure vanilla
    extract

4 Twinkies, broken into
    1-inch pieces

In a small bowl, combine the flour and cold water and stir until a smooth paste forms. Prepare a double boiler over simmering water.

Pour the milk into a saucepan and heat over low heat until warm. And the flour paste and blend well. Cook, stirring constantly, for about 15 minutes, until the milk is hot and slightly thickened. Transfer the mixture to the top of the double boiler and cook, stirring frequently, for 15 minutes, until bubbles start to form around the edges. Don't let it come to a full boil. Stir in the sugar.

Blend a small amount of the hot milk mixture into the beaten egg yolks. Then blend all of the egg yolk mixture back into the hot milk mixture. Cook, stirring constantly, for 2 minutes. Pass the custard through a fine-mesh sieve into a bowl. Cover and refrigerate for 1 to 2 hours, until well chilled.

Stir the cream and vanilla into the custard mixture. Transfer to a 2-quart ice cream maker and freeze according to the manufacturer's instructions. When the ice cream is almost frozen, stir in the Twinkie pieces. Freeze until firm.

GRANDMA JO'S TWINKIE JELL-O DESSERT

6 6 This dessert dates back to the 1960s, when my Grandma Jo would make it for special occasions. I've had a framed copy of the recipe in her original handwriting hanging in my kitchen for years. It's the ultimate comfort food and the source of many special happy memories. 9 9

MARY CAINE, HUDSON, OHIO

SERVES 12

10 Twinkies

2 (3-ounce) packages orange Jell-O

1 cup boiling water

1 (20-ounce) can crushed pineapple in juice, drained

1 cup lemon-lime soda

1 quart vanilla ice cream, at room temperature

Arrange the Twinkies in the bottom of a 9 by 13-inch baking dish.

In a bowl, mix together the Jell-O and boiling water, stirring until dissolved. Stir in the pineapple and soda. Blend in the ice cream and beat until smooth with a whisk or an electric mixer on low speed. Pour the Jell-O mixture over the Twinkies and refrigerate for 2 to 3 hours, until set.

To serve, cut into squares and serve chilled.

CHAPTER SIX

TWINKIE
DRINKS

TWINKIE LOVE POTION NUMBER 75

This Hostess original recipe for a smoothie beverage was created to commemorate Twinkies' seventy-fifth anniversary. It's best served parlor style, with two straws!

SERVES 2

2 Twinkies
2 scoops vanilla ice cream
1 cup strawberries

In a blender, combine the Twinkies with the ice cream and strawberries and blend until smooth. Pour into a tall glass and serve immediately.

TWINKIE MILKSHAKE

66 *I created this special family recipe on a whim. My daughter, Sarah, would always dunk Twinkies in chocolate milkshakes. So one day, I made her a chocolate shake and added Twinkies to it. It is still one of her—and the rest of the family's—favorites.* 99

BRENDA McDEVITT, WORTH, ILLINOIS

SERVES 2

2 Twinkies
2 scoops chocolate ice cream
1 cup milk
Whipped cream, for topping

In a blender, combine the Twinkies, ice cream, and milk and process until smooth. Pour into a tall glass and top with a dollop of whipped cream. Serve at once.

TWINKIE GRASSHOPPER

" My family loves chocolate and mint together. When we make shakes, we like to thicken them up with cakes and cookies. Twinkies just seemed to be the perfect complement to our grasshopper concoction. "

LORI KIMBLE, MASCOUTAH, ILLINOIS

SERVES 3 TO 4

2 1/3 cups milk

6 Twinkies

4 chocolate-covered mint cookies

2 tablespoons chocolate syrup

3 cups vanilla ice cream

In a blender, combine 2 cups of the milk and the Twinkies and blend for 5 to 10 seconds. Add the cookies and syrup and blend until smooth, then add the ice cream and blend until smooth once again. Pour in the remaining 1/3 cup milk and blend until thoroughly mixed. Serve at once.

CHAPTER SEVEN

TWINKIE
STACK-UPS

PATRIOTIC TWINKIE PIE

66 *While preparing a recipe for a Fourth of July party, I realized I was missing a few key ingredients. It was too late to go to the store, so I began looking for substitutes and used some of the Twinkies I had on hand. Twinkies gave the dessert a distinctive taste, and I've never gone back to the old recipe!* *99*

RUTH ROYAL, CODY, WYOMING

SERVES 16

1 (6-ounce) package
    blueberry Jell-O

3 cups boiling water

1 (16-ounce) bag frozen
    blueberries

1 (6-ounce) package
    strawberry Jell-O

1 (16-ounce) bag frozen sliced
    strawberries in syrup

6 to 7 Twinkies, broken or
    torn into 1-inch pieces

2 (5.1-ounce) packages instant
    vanilla pudding mix

6 cups milk

1 (12-ounce) container frozen
    nondairy whipped
    topping, thawed

In a bowl, combine the blueberry Jell-O and 1 1/2 cups of the boiling water and stir until dissolved. Add the blueberries and stir until blended and slightly thickened. Allow to cool completely.

In another bowl, combine the strawberry Jell-O and remaining 1 1/2 cups boiling water and stir until dissolved. Add the strawberries and stir until blended and slightly thickened. Allow to cool completely.

Place half of the Twinkie pieces in a 6-quart glass bowl or trifle dish. In a separate bowl, combine the pudding mix and milk and stir according to the package instructions. Spoon half of the pudding over the Twinkies.

Spoon the blueberry mixture over the pudding, spreading evenly. Top with the remaining Twinkie pieces. Spoon the remaining pudding over the Twinkies, spreading evenly. Spoon the strawberry mixture over the pudding, spreading evenly.

Cover and refrigerate for several hours or overnight, until completely chilled and set. Top with the whipped topping just before serving.

PEANUT BUTTER AND JELLY TWINKIE CAKE

This recipe was a spur-of-the-moment idea. I created it because I knew my nine grandchildren would like it. Making this cake is something we can all do together. I also serve it at potlucks and church functions.

DONNA SPROUSE, ORDWAY, COLORADO

SERVES 9

10 Twinkies

1/2 cup raspberry jelly

2 (3.4-ounce) packages instant vanilla pudding mix

3 cups milk

1/2 cup peanut butter

1 cup frozen nondairy whipped topping, thawed

Cut 5 of the Twinkies in half lengthwise and arrange them cut side up in the bottom of a 9 by 9-inch baking dish.

Warm the raspberry jelly in a small saucepan over low heat until soft enough to spread easily, about 2 minutes. Spread the warm jelly over the Twinkies.

In a bowl, combine the pudding mix, milk, and peanut butter and mix well. Pour over the Twinkies in the pan. Cut the remaining 5 Twinkies in half lengthwise and place cut side down on top of the pudding.

Refrigerate for at least 1 hour. Garnish with dollops of whipped topping before cutting into squares to serve.

STRAWBERRY TWINKIE STACK

66 *I've been making this dessert for twenty years, and it's always a hit at parties and family gatherings. A few years ago, my brother asked me to make it for him. I thought he wanted to take it to work, but instead he took it to church. A few days later my phone was ringing off the hook with parishioners looking for the recipe.* 99

MARY BENNETT, KELLER, TEXAS

SERVES 10 TO 15

1 (5.1-ounce) package instant vanilla pudding mix

3 cups milk

1/2 to 1 cup Kahlúa, sherry, or pure peach juice

20 Twinkies

3 to 4 cups sliced fresh strawberries

1 cup heavy whipping cream, whipped until stiff peaks form

1/2 cup sliced almonds

Chopped maraschino cherries, for garnish

In a bowl, combine the pudding mix and milk and stir according to the package instructions.

Pour the Kahlúa into a shallow dish. Dip 10 of the Twinkies into the Kahlúa, so the long bottom half of each is submerged. Arrange the Twinkies dipped side down across the bottom and up the sides of a 5- to 6-quart trifle bowl or deep glass bowl.

Spread one-third of the pudding evenly over the Twinkies. Top with one-third of the strawberries and one-third of the whipped cream, spreading evenly. Sprinkle with one-third of the almonds.

Repeat the Kahlúa-dipping procedure with 5 more Twinkies. Arrange the Twinkies over the almonds, then layer with another one-third of the pudding, strawberries, whipped cream, and almonds. Repeat the Kahlúa-dipping procedure with the remaining 5 Twinkies, then repeat the layering of Twinkies, pudding, strawberries, whipped cream, and almonds, using up all of those ingredients.

Cover and refrigerate overnight. Garnish with the cherries just before serving.

TWINKIE LASAGNA

When I was a child, my mother always packed Twinkies in my lunch. As I matured, I wanted to incorporate my fondness for Twinkies into an adult treat. People love it when I make this dessert; it brings back sweet memories.

DIANA PILLITTIERI, JAMESTOWN, NEW YORK

SERVES 12

10 Twinkies, halved lengthwise

1 (12-ounce) bag semisweet or milk chocolate chips

1 cup sliced fresh strawberries

1 cup fresh raspberries

1 (3.4-ounce) package instant vanilla pudding mix

2 cups milk

1 (8-ounce) container frozen nondairy whipped topping, thawed

Arrange the Twinkies cut side up in a 9 by 13-inch baking dish.

Place the chocolate chips in a microwave-safe bowl and microwave on high power for 1 minute. Stir and continue to microwave for 15 to 30 seconds, stirring frequently, until melted and smooth. Drizzle the chocolate over the Twinkies, then layer the strawberries and raspberries over the chocolate.

In a bowl, combine the pudding mix and milk and stir according to the package instructions, until thickened. Pour the pudding over the fruit, then spoon the whipped topping over the pudding. Refrigerate for 2 to 3 hours, until set.

TRIFLE IN THE TWINKIE OF AN EYE

" *I originally developed this recipe because my son is addicted to Twinkies. I wanted to let him have his favorite cake but also give him the benefits of fresh fruit. We really like this cool dessert in the summer, because fruits are abundant and you don't have to heat up the kitchen. As an added benefit, it carries well in a cooler to a picnic or potluck.* "

MARLA HYATT, SAINT PAUL, MINNESOTA

SERVES 10 TO 12

12 Twinkies

2 cups fresh strawberries, quartered

1 (8-ounce) container extra creamy frozen nondairy whipped topping, thawed

2 peaches, peeled and cut into bite-size cubes

2 cups fresh blueberries

2 bananas

2 tablespoons freshly squeezed lemon juice

1/4 cup chopped macadamia nuts

Cut each Twinkie into 6 pieces. Layer one-third of the Twinkies in a 3-quart trifle bowl or a deep glass bowl. Top with the strawberries, then top with one-third of the whipped topping. Top with another one-third of the Twinkies, then top with the peaches and another one-third of the whipped topping. Top with the remaining Twinkies, then top with the blueberries and the remaining whipped topping.

Slice the bananas and rinse quickly in the lemon juice to prevent darkening. Drain well. Arrange the banana slices over the whipped topping and sprinkle with the nuts. Cover and refrigerate for at least 2 hours and up to 12 hours. Serve well chilled.

CHAPTER EIGHT

GOURMET
TWINKIES

TWINKIE-MISU

66 *When my sister returned from living in Italy for a time, she grew homesick for the desserts she had enjoyed there. So I decided to try my hand at tiramisu, but replaced the ladyfingers with Twinkies, which we had all grown up on. She liked it just as much as the original!* 99

ZEPHIR PLUME, BOULDER, COLORADO

SERVES 6 TO 8

1 (3.4-ounce) package instant vanilla pudding mix

1³/₄ cups milk

¹/₄ cup Amaretto

1 cup strong coffee, warmed

1 tablespoon sugar

¹/₄ cup Kahlúa

2 cups frozen nondairy whipped topping, thawed

10 Twinkies

Unsweetened cocoa, for dusting

In a bowl, combine the pudding mix, milk, and Amaretto and whisk. Set aside until quite thick.

In a separate, small bowl, combine the coffee, sugar, and Kahlúa and mix until the sugar dissolves. Refrigerate until cool. Line a baking sheet with waxed paper and set the Twinkies on the paper. Slowly drizzle the coffee mixture over each Twinkie, allowing the liquid to soak in.

Fold the whipped topping into the pudding mixture. Spoon one-third of the pudding mixture into an 8 by 8-inch baking dish.

Arrange the Twinkies evenly over the pudding. Spoon the remaining pudding over the Twinkies.

Refrigerate for 1 hour, or until set. Dust with cocoa just before serving.

BANANA TWINKIE BREAD PUDDING

This recipe can also be flambéed: Place the rum and liqueur in a long, heatproof ladle and carefully light it with a long match. Pour the flaming spirits into the banana mixture and shake the skillet gently until the flame subsides.

DIANE HALFERTY, CORPUS CHRISTI, TEXAS

SERVES 12

10 Twinkies, cut into bite-size pieces

3 cups milk

3 eggs

2/3 cup sugar

2 very ripe large bananas

1 tablespoon ground cinnamon

1/4 teaspoon ground nutmeg

1/2 teaspoon pure vanilla extract

1/2 cup dried cherries or sweetened dried cranberries

1/2 cup pecans, lightly toasted

3 tablespoons unsalted butter, cut into small pieces

Preheat the oven to 300°F. Butter a 9 by 13-inch baking dish. Place the Twinkie pieces in a large bowl.

In a blender, combine the milk, eggs, sugar, bananas, cinnamon, nutmeg, and vanilla and process until smooth. Pour over the Twinkie pieces. Fold in the cherries and pecans. Transfer the mixture to the prepared baking dish and let stand for 20 minutes. Top with the butter.

Cover the baking dish with aluminum foil and place it into a larger pan. Put the pans in the oven and pour hot water into the larger pan to a depth of 1 inch. Bake for 1 hour, then remove the foil and bake uncovered for 15 to 20 minutes, until a knife inserted just off center comes out clean.

To prepare the topping, whisk or beat the cream in a bowl just until it begins to thicken. Add the sugar

TOPPING

3/4 cup heavy whipping
  cream

1 tablespoon sugar

1/4 teaspoon pure vanilla
  extract

SAUCE

2/3 cup unsalted butter,
  at room temperature

1/2 cup packed light brown
  sugar

6 large ripe bananas, sliced

1 teaspoon ground cinnamon

1/4 teaspoon ground nutmeg

3 tablespoons dark rum, or
  1 tablespoon rum extract

2 tablespoons banana
  liqueur or strawberry-
  banana juice

1 teaspoon pure vanilla
  extract

and vanilla and continue beating until soft peaks form. Cover and refrigerate.

To prepare the sauce, heat a large sauté pan or skillet over low heat. Add the butter and brown sugar and cook, stirring gently, until melted and smooth. Add the bananas, cinnamon, and nutmeg and cook for 1 to 2 minutes, until the bananas just begin to soften. Stir very gently so as not to break up the bananas. Remove the pan from the heat and add the rum and liqueur. Return the pan to the heat, add the vanilla, and stir well. Remove from heat and keep warm.

To serve, place a large scoop of the Twinkie pudding in the middle of each plate or bowl. Spoon some sauce over each piece. Top with the whipped cream and serve immediately.

TWINKIE-PECAN BANANAS FOSTER

As a kid at soccer camp, I lived on Twinkies. After becoming a professional chef, I started looking at ways to do new things with old confections. For Twinkies, I wanted to do something dramatic—an avant-garde take on the most old-school dessert around.

NOLAN STUDLEY, NEW YORK, NEW YORK

SERVES 4

2 bananas, halved lengthwise

2 Twinkies, halved lengthwise, well chilled

1/4 cup butter

1 cup packed dark brown sugar

1 teaspoon ground allspice

1/4 cup banana liqueur

1/2 cup dark rum

1/4 cup pecan halves or pieces

1 teaspoon ground cinnamon

2 cups vanilla ice cream

Cut the banana pieces and the Twinkie pieces in half crosswise.

Melt the butter in a skillet over medium-high heat. Add the brown sugar and allspice and stir to form a thick paste. Cook, stirring occasionally, for about 5 minutes, until the mixture caramelizes.

Stir in the banana liqueur and rum. Heat for about 3 minutes, until the spirits are warmed. Add the bananas, Twinkies, and pecans and cook for 1 to 2 minutes. Remove the pan from the heat and carefully ignite the mixture with a long match. Sprinkle the cinnamon over the flames for a sparkling effect.

Scoop the ice cream into 4 individual dessert bowls. Ladle the warm Twinkie mixture over the ice cream and serve at once.

PUMPKIN TWINKIE BREAD PUDDING

" *This recipe makes the house smell yummy in the fall and winter. As an added bonus, the scent of pumpkin is an aphrodisiac for men!* "

SORAYA HAMID, KANSAS CITY, MISSOURI

SERVES 6

1 cup canned pumpkin purée
2 large eggs, lightly beaten
1 egg yolk, lightly beaten
1 cup milk
1 tablespoon molasses
1/4 cup sugar
1 teaspoon pure vanilla extract
1/2 teaspoon ground ginger
1/2 teaspoon ground cinnamon
Pinch of salt
5 Twinkies, cubed

CARAMEL SAUCE

1 cup sugar
2 tablespoons freshly
  squeezed lemon juice
1/2 cup cold water

Preheat the oven to 350°F. Butter 6 six-ounce ramekins.

In a bowl, whisk together the pumpkin, eggs, egg yolk, milk, molasses, sugar, vanilla, ginger, cinnamon, and salt. Divide the Twinkie cubes among the ramekins, then pour the pumpkin mixture over the Twinkies. Let sit for about 10 minutes, until the Twinkies have absorbed the liquid.

Place the ramekins in a roasting pan and place the pan in the oven. Pour enough warm water into the pan to reach halfway up the sides of the ramekins. Bake for about 40 minutes, until the puddings are brown and the centers have set. Remove from the oven and allow to cool for 10 minutes.

To prepare the sauce, first fill a large bowl with ice water. In a small saucepan over medium heat, combine the sugar and lemon juice. Cover and cook for 3 to 5 minutes, until the sugar has melted. Uncover and continue cooking for 5 to 7 minutes, swirling the pan occasionally, until the sugar turns a deep amber color. Plunge the bottom of the pan into the prepared bowl of ice water to stop the cooking process. Wearing oven mitts, carefully pour in the 1/2 cup cold water, being careful not to splatter. Stir frequently until ready to use.

To serve, turn the puddings out on to dessert plates. Spoon some caramel sauce over each and serve at once.

TWINKIES
AND MEAT

CHICKEN-RASPBERRY TWINKIE SALAD

> *I often try to create new recipes from odds and ends that I have in the refrigerator and that's how this dish came about. I was out of Wonder Bread one day and improvised using Twinkies. It turned out great. I am a former Peace Corps volunteer who has served in several Latin American countries, so making do with things and survival-style preparation come naturally to me.*

GARY GONYA, BALTIMORE, MARYLAND

SERVES 6

- 1/2 cup raspberry preserves
- 1/4 cup balsamic vinegar
- 6 Twinkies, halved lengthwise
- 2 cups shredded cooked chicken
- 2 Roma tomatoes, seeded and diced
- 1 fresh jalapeño pepper, seeded and diced
- 2 tablespoons chopped red onion
- Salt and freshly ground black pepper
- 1 cup shredded cheddar cheese
- 2 cups mixed baby greens

Preheat the oven to 450°F.

In a small bowl, whisk together 1/4 cup of the raspberry preserves and 2 tablespoons of the vinegar to make a raspberry vinaigrette. Set aside.

With a small spoon, scrape the filling out of the Twinkies and reserve in a bowl. Place the Twinkies cut side up on a baking sheet.

Add the remaining 1/4 cup raspberry preserves and 2 tablespoons vinegar to the reserved crème filling. Mix until well blended, then add the chicken and mix well.

In a separate bowl, combine the tomatoes, jalapeño, and onion and mix well. Season to taste with salt and pepper.

Place a spoonful of the chicken mixture in each

Twinkie half. Sprinkle the cheese over the Twinkies, dividing evenly. Spoon the tomato mixture over the top, dividing evenly.

Place in the oven and bake for about 5 minutes, until the cheese melts. Arrange a bed of the mixed greens on each of 6 plates. Remove the Twinkies from the oven and place 2 halves on each bed of greens. Drizzle with the raspberry vinaigrette and serve immediately.

PIGS IN A TWINKIE

❝ *My twelve-year-old nephew Shea created this recipe because he thought it would be something other kids would enjoy. It's important to make sure that the sausage is cooked thoroughly.* ❞

JANINE O'BARR, BURBANK, CALIFORNIA

SERVES 6

6 pork sausage links
6 Twinkies
Maple syrup, for serving

Preheat the oven to 350°F.

Place the sausage in a skillet over medium heat and cook, turning to brown evenly, until the meat is no longer pink inside, following any package directions. Remove from the skillet and drain well on paper towels.

Thinly slice one end off each Twinkie. Stuff a cooked sausage into each Twinkie. Place the Twinkies in a shallow baking dish and bake for 10 minutes, or until the Twinkies are warm. Serve warm, with syrup.

TWINKLING TURKEY

66 *I have always loved to cook and experiment often. I came up with this new twist on an old favorite for my boyfriend, who loves Twinkies. Although I have no children, my nieces spend weekends with me and we often cook together. I want them to learn how to cook with different ingredients than what is considered standard. Adding Twinkies to an entrée is one of those unusual combinations that worked out very well indeed!* 99

CAROL MACOMBER, BELVIDERE, ILLINOIS

SERVES 15 TO 20

1 (8¹/₂-ounce) package yellow corn muffin mix, prepared and baked according to package instructions

6 Twinkies, halved lengthwise

1 (14- to 18-pound) turkey

1 tart apple, peeled, cored, and diced

¹/₄ cup honey

Remove the muffins from the oven and allow to cool on a wire rack.

Preheat the oven to 350°F. Scrape the crème filling out of the Twinkies with a small spoon and reserve in a small bowl.

Cut the Twinkie pastry into cubes and spread in a single layer on a baking sheet. Bake for 8 to 10 minutes, until lightly toasted. Remove from the oven and allow to cool completely. Decrease the oven temperature to 325°F.

Rinse the turkey. Crumble the muffins into a bowl, add the apple and toasted Twinkies, and mix lightly. Loosely stuff the mixture into the turkey and truss the legs. Place the turkey, breast side up, on a rack set in a roasting pan. Roast the turkey for 12 to 15 minutes per pound, until the thigh temperature reaches 175°F to 180°F and the juices run clear.

In a small bowl, combine the honey with the reserved crème filling and mix well. Brush the turkey with the honey mixture during the last 10 to 15 minutes of roasting time.

Remove the turkey from the oven and let stand for 20 minutes before carving.

INDEX

Bananas
  Banana Frozen Yogurt Twinkie Sundae, 58
  Banana Twinkie Bread Pudding, 87–88
  Trifle in the Twinkie of an Eye, 82
  Twinkie Banana Split, 60
  Twinkie-Choconana Toffee Crunch, 27
  Twinkie-Pecan Bananas Foster, 89
Blueberries
  Patriotic Twinkie Pie, 75–76
  Trifle in the Twinkie of an Eye, 82
Browning, Lewis, 6–7
Burrito, Twinkie, 29

Cakes
  Easy Twinkie Peach Cake, 50
  Peanut Butter and Jelly Twinkie Cake, 77
  Ribbons and Bows Twinkie Wedding Cake,
    46–48
  Twinkie Cheesecake with Cherry
    Topping, 54
  Twinkie Icebox Cake, 55
  Twinkie Ice Cream Cake, 59
  Twinkie Macchiato Cake, 51
  Twinkie Tunnel Bundt Cake, 53
Cheesecake, Twinkie, with Cherry Topping, 54

Cherries
  Banana Twinkie Bread Pudding, 87–88
  Twinkie Cheesecake with Cherry
    Topping, 54
  Twinkie Cherry Pie, 43
Chicken-Raspberry Twinkie Salad, 95–96
Chocolate
  Chocolate Twinkie Pops, 34
  Chocolate Twinkie Trifle, 30
  Fried Twinkies with Chocolate Sauce, 26
  Twinkie Birds, 14–15
  Twinkie Burrito, 29
  Twinkie-Choconana Toffee Crunch, 27
  Twinkie Easter Egg Hunt, 18
  Twinkie Éclair, 31
  Twinkie Grasshopper, 70
  Twinkiehenge, 20
  Twinkie Ice Cream Cake, 59
  Twinkie Lasagna, 80
  Twinkie Macchiato Cake, 51
  Twinkie Milkshake, 69
  Twinkie Peanut Butter Logs, 13
  Twinkie Petits Fours, 32
  Twinkie Train, 12
  Twinkie Tunnel Bundt Cake, 53

Coffee
    Twinkie Macchiato Cake, 51
    Twinkie-Misu, 84
Cream cheese
    Twinkie Cheesecake with Cherry Topping, 54
    Twinkie Cherry Pie, 43

Deep-Fried Twinkies with Raspberry Syrup,
    22–23
Dewar, James A., 4–6
Drinks
    Twinkie Grasshopper, 70
    Twinkie Love Potion Number 75, 68
    Twinkie Milkshake, 69

Easter Egg Hunt, Twinkie, 18
Easy Twinkie Peach Cake, 50
Éclair, Twinkie, 31

French Twinkies, 21
Fried Twinkies with Chocolate Sauce, 26
Fruit. See also individual fruits
    Twinkie Kebabals, 37
    Twinkie Sushi, 10

Grandma Jo's Twinkie Jell-O Dessert, 66

Ice cream
    Grandma Jo's Twinkie Jell-O Dessert, 66
    Twinkie Banana Split, 60
    Twinkie Bomb, 63
    Twinkie Grasshopper, 70
    Twinkie Ice Cream, 64–65
    Twinkie Ice Cream Cake, 59
    Twinkie Love Potion Number 75, 68

    Twinkie Milkshake, 69
    Twinkie-Pecan Bananas Foster, 89

Jell-O
    Grandma Jo's Twinkie Jell-O Dessert, 66
    Patriotic Twinkie Pie, 75–76
    Twinkie Fantasy, 40
    Twinkie Orange Bavarian Dream, 41

Lasagna, Twinkie, 80

Marshmallows and marshmallow crème
    Twinkie Easter Egg Hunt, 18
    Twinkie Kebabals, 37
    Twinkie Macchiato Cake, 51

Orange Bavarian Dream, Twinkie, 41

Pancakes, Twinkie, 17
Patriotic Twinkie Pie, 75–76
Peaches
    Easy Twinkie Peach Cake, 50
    Trifle in the Twinkie of an Eye, 82
Peanut butter
    Peanut Butter and Jelly Twinkie Cake, 77
    Twinkie Peanut Butter Logs, 13
Petits Fours, Twinkie, 32
Pie, Twinkie Cherry, 43
Pigs in a Twinkie, 97
Pineapple
    Grandma Jo's Twinkie Jell-O Dessert, 66
    Pineapple Twinkie Pudding, 44
    Twinkie Banana Split, 60
    Twinkie Cherry Pie, 43
    Twinkie Icebox Cake, 55

Pops, Chocolate Twinkie, 34
Pudding
    Banana Twinkie Bread Pudding, 87–88
    Chocolate Twinkie Trifle, 30
    Patriotic Twinkie Pie, 75–76
    Peanut Butter and Jelly Twinkie Cake, 77
    Pineapple Twinkie Pudding, 44
    Pumpkin Twinkie Bread Pudding, 90–91
    Strawberry Twinkie Stack, 78–79
    Twinkie-Choconana Toffee Crunch, 27
    Twinkie Easter Egg Hunt, 18
    Twinkie Éclair, 31
    Twinkie Fantasy, 40
    Twinkiehenge, 20
    Twinkie Icebox Cake, 55
    Twinkie Lasagna, 80
    Twinkie-Misu, 84
    Twinkie Orange Bavarian Dream, 41
Pumpkin Twinkie Bread Pudding, 90–91

Raspberries
    Chicken-Raspberry Twinkie Salad, 95–96
    Deep-Fried Twinkies with Raspberry
        Syrup, 22–23
    Peanut Butter and Jelly Twinkie Cake, 77
    Twinkie Bomb, 63
    Twinkie Lasagna, 80
Ribbons and Bows Twinkie Wedding Cake,
    46–48

Salad, Chicken-Raspberry Twinkie, 95–96
Sausage
    Pigs in a Twinkie, 97
Shortcake, Twinkie Strawberry, 38

Strawberries
    Patriotic Twinkie Pie, 75–76
    Strawberry Twinkie Stack, 78–79
    Trifle in the Twinkie of an Eye, 82
    Twinkie Banana Split, 60
    Twinkie Burrito, 29
    Twinkie Fantasy, 40
    Twinkie Lasagna, 80
    Twinkie Love Potion Number 75, 68
    Twinkie Strawberry Shortcake, 38
Sundae, Banana Frozen Yogurt Twinkie, 58
Sushi, Twinkie, 10

Tortillas
    Twinkie Burrito, 29
Trifles
    Chocolate Twinkie Trifle, 30
    Patriotic Twinkie Pie, 75–76
    Trifle in the Twinkie of an Eye, 82
Turkey, Twinkling, 98–99
Twinkies
    calories in, 3
    history of, 3–8
    as national icon, 1–2
    shelf life of, 2
Twinkling Turkey, 98–99

Yogurt Twinkie Sundae, Banana Frozen, 58